BUMPER
HOT JOKES
FOR KOOL KIDS
VOLUME TWO

COMPILED BY
Andy Jones

ILLUSTRATED BY
Stephen Axelsen

ABC
BOOKS

Acknowledgments

Many thanks to all the kool kids from the following kool schools who contributed jokes to this book:

Allanson PS

Allenswood PS

Ashford Central School

Augusta PS

Australind PS

Beachlands PS

Bethany College Kogarah

Beverley DHS

Boyanup PS

Boyup Brook DHS

Bridgetown Primary School and
   Lisa Field

Busselton West PS

Cloverdale PS

Collie Catholic College

Dandaragan PS

Darkan DHS

Dunsborough PS

Flinders Park PS

Gingin DHS

Katanning PS

Korakonui School

Mandurah North PS

Merredin North PS

Merredin South PS

Moora PS

Morawa DHS

Narrogin PS

Pemberton DHS

Petersham Kindergarten

Petersham PS

Port Kennedy PS

Rostrata PS

Taverners Hill PS

Vasse PS

Victoria Park PS

Wilson Park PS

Woodanilling PS

York DHS

Contents

Odds 'n' Ends

*A bit of this
And that, my friends
A funny lot of
Odds 'n' Ends*

Q. Who's your best friend at school?

A. **Your Princi-pal**   Stacey J. aged 9

Q. What did the hat say to the scarf?

A. **You hang around and I'll go ahead**   Nick B. aged 9

Q. What are hundreds and thousands?

A. **Smarty droppings** Caris B. aged 10

Q. What sort of vegetables do athletes prefer?

A. **Runner beans**
Marnie B. aged 8

Q. Who is the best underwater spy?

A. **James Pond**
Ben J. aged 10

Q. Why shouldn't you tell secrets to a clock?

A. **Because time will always tell** Alex H. aged 10

Q. What did the dentist say to his wife when she baked a cake?

A. **Can I do the filling?** Charlee C. aged 8

Q. Why was Mr Maths upset?

A. **Because his son was a problem** Amber C. aged 12

Q. Why was Cinderella thrown off the netball team?

A. **Because she kept running away from the ball**
Mathew R. aged 11

Animal
Magnetism

They're regal, majestic
And love to run free
Animal Magnetism
Is something to see

Q. What do you get if you cross a mouse with a pip?

A. **A pip-squeak**
Natasha. S. aged 10

Q. What do sheep eat?

A. **Chocolate baas**
Fiona F. aged 11

Q. What do you call a sheep in a bikini?

A. **Bra Bra Black Sheep**
Joel G. aged 6

Q. Why couldn't the pony talk?

A. **'Cause he was a little horse**
Nelly N. aged 6

Q. What do geese do in traffic jams?

A. **They honk**
Keely R.R. aged 12

HONK
HONK

8

Q. What do you call a woodpecker without a beak?

A. A head banger Marli H. aged 10

Q. What do you call a bunch of tweety birds?

A. A squawkestra Kelly P. aged 8

Q. Where do rabbits go when they get married?

A. On a bunny moon Sarah D. aged 6

Q. What do you get when you walk under a cow?

A. A pat on the head
Renee W. aged 12

Q. What do you get when you tickle a cow?

A. A good kick out of it Lynette A. aged 10

Q. What do you call a cow that eats grass?

A. **A lawn mooer** Leathan S. aged 7

Q. How does a farmer count his cows?

A. **With a cowculator** Louise J. aged 8

Q. Did you hear about the Frenchman who hated snails?

A. **He liked fast food**
James M. aged 9

Q. Why did the bees go on strike?

A. **They wanted shorter flowers and more honey**
Kerry R. aged 10

Q. How do fish go into business?

A. **They start small-scale**
Geoffrey A.R. aged 11

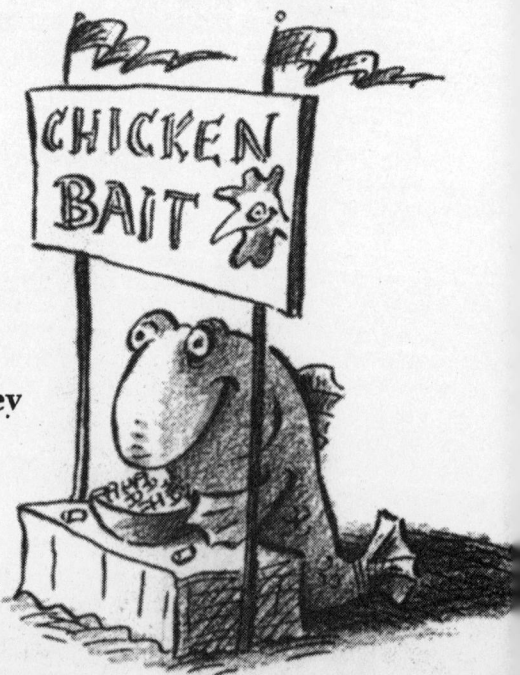

Q. What type of fur do you get from a brown bear?

A. **As fur away as possible**   Lathan W. aged 6

Q. What do you call a white bear who loves to lie in the sun listening to pop music, rolling balls and drinking soft drink?

A. **A solar, roller, bowler, cola-polar**
Felicity W. aged 11

Q. What do you get if you cross a hyena with a shark?

A. **I don't know, but if it laughs I'll join in**
Randall S. aged 6

Q. What did the dinosaur say when it saw the volcano erupt?

A. **What a lava-ly day**   Daniel E. aged 10

Batty Blunders

Moonlit nights
And cracking thunder
Vampire jokes and
Batty Blunders

Q. Why is it easy to trick a vampire?

A. **Because they're all suckers**   Robbie S. aged 7

Q. What do you call a vampire's dog?

A. **A blood hound**   Ashley D. aged 9

Q. What do vampires use to catch fish?

A. **Bloodworms**   Kevin C. aged 12

Q. What kind of ships do vampires sail?

A. **Blood vessels**   Greta P. aged 6

Q. What happens when you upset a vampire?

A. **He sees red**   Arnold J. aged 11

Q. What type of girls do vampires like?

A. **Red heads**   Tricia M. aged 6

Q. What do you call vampire twins?

A. **Blood brothers**   Kevin C. aged 12

Q. Where do vampires go for holidays?

A. **Batavia**   Collin P. aged 12

Q. What do vampires bath in?

A. **A bloodbath**   Terri W. aged 8

Q. When is a vampire a super hero?

A. **When he's Batman**
Allicia C. aged 7

Star Struck

They shoot through the sky
So get ready to duck
If you gaze too deeply
You'll become Star Struck!

Q. What sort of star is dangerous?

A. **A shooting star**

Maree D. aged 9

Q. What do you call a famous rock?

A. **A rock star**

Kent B. aged 10

Q. What do you call a young star?

A. **A grommit-comet**
Dale S. aged 10

Q. How do you get a baby astronaut to sleep?

A. **Rocket**
Chloe M.D. aged 10

Q. What happened to the two planets that collided?

A. **They were star-tled**
Virginia Q. aged 11

Q. What do you call an intergalactic garbage truck?

A. **A dump-star**
Angelo M. aged 10

Q. What star only comes out on Mondays?

A. **A mon-star**   Nick Joseph aged 35, Jacaranda Retirement Home

Q. What do you call the referee at a cosmic athletics meeting?

A. **The star-ter**   Angela L. aged 12

Q. What did the alien say to the plant?

A. **Take me to your weeder**   Carl K. aged 9

bananarama

They're bright and yellow
And nothing like llamas
We all eat them
They're called Bananas

Q. What do you say to a frozen banana?

A. **Cool banana**   Lisa R. aged 11

Q. What do you call a sunburnt banana?

A   **A banana peel**   Genna S. aged 8

Q. What do
bananas
wear for
underwear?

A. **I don't know,
peel one
and see**
Kelvin J.
aged 10

Q. Why is a banana skin like a T-shirt?

A. **Because it's easy to slip on**
Marnie B. aged 8

Q. What do you call a sheep that eats bananas?

A. **A Baa-Baa-nana**
Andrew P. aged 9

Can-tankerous

Some hold spaghetti
Some hold ham
There's nothing quite like
The humble tin can!

Q. What's a can's favourite card game?

A. **Canasta**

Lenny P. aged 9

Q. What's yellow, made of steel and can fly?

A. **A canary**
Courtney L. aged 9

Q. What's a can's favourite dance?

A. **The Can Can**
Trent T. aged 8

Q. What's a can's best friend?

A. **Rin Tin Tin**   Lenny P. aged 9

Q. What do you get if you cross a can with a poodle?

A. **A can-noodle**   Trent T. aged 8

Q. What's a can's favourite music?

A. **Heavy metal**   Lilly A. aged 8

Q. What do you call a can with a sweet tooth?

A. **Candy**   John H. aged 8

Q. When is a can not a can?

A. **When it's uncanny**   Allivia S. aged 5

Q. Where do cans go for their holidays?

A. **Canada**   Eva H. aged 8

Q. What do you call a can that takes pictures?

A. A handy-can   Ellen G. aged 9

Q. What do you get if you cross a bird with a can?

A. A tou-can   Elliot W. aged 8

It's not ham and eggs
Or bacon from porkers
It's a whole
new section
Of roaring Ripsnorters!

ripsnorters

OINK OINK OINK OINK

Q. How do pigs get to hospital?

A. **In a hambulance**   Greg P. aged 6

Q. What do you call a greedy pig?

A. **A hog**   Allan T. aged 7

To eat or not to eat? That is the question. Whether 'tis nobler for the swine...

Q. What do you call a theatrical pig?

A. **Hamlet**
Mark A. aged 8

Q. Where do pigs go for their holidays?

A. **Hamsterdam**
Mary W. aged 7

Q. What's a pig's favourite sport?

A. **Hamball**
Melanie F. aged 8

Q. What does a pig call his grandfather?

A **Hampa**
Tristen G. aged 6

Q. What do pigs call second-hand clothes?

A. **Ham-me-downs**
Petra T. aged 7

Terrific Tomatoes

They're red and juicy
They squirt up your nose!
Those squishy, delishy
Terrific Tomatoes

Q. What's red, round and juicy, and has toes but no feet?

A. **Tomatoes**
Caplan W. aged 10

Q. What did the police do to the suspicious tomato?

A. **They grilled him** Simon R. aged 7

Q. When does a tomato become another vegetable?

A. **When it gets squashed** Mavis B. aged 9

Q. What's better than one tomato?

A. **To-matoes** Nick L. aged 8

Q. What do you call a sunburnt potato?

A. **A tomato** Gill G. aged 9

I Knew That

They always say it
Right off the bat
"I told you so"
"I knew that"

Q. Why did the toilet paper roll down the hill?

A. **To get to the bottom**   Bradley M. aged 9

Q. Where does a snowman dance?

A. **At a snow ball**   Kasey O. aged 11

Q. What do you call a pair of underwear thieves?

A. **A pair of knickers!**   Kylie V. aged 8

Q. What sort of biscuits can fly?

A. **Plain biscuits**
Jessica M. aged 1

Q. What gets bigger the more you take away?

A. **A hole**   Matthew T. aged 8

Q. What kind of pliers do you use in maths?

A. **Multipliers**   Erica T. aged 11

Q. What gets wet as it dries?

A. **A towel**   Michelle J. aged 9

Q. Why did the girl throw her toast out of the window?

A. **She wanted to see the butterfly**
Ashlee R. aged 10

Q. What three letters are robbers scared of?

A. **I.C.U.** Regina W. aged 9

Q. Why was Isaac Newton, the mathematics genius, surprised when he was hit on the head by an apple?

A. **He was sitting under a pear tree** Janelle P. aged 11

Q. What banks never run out of money?

A. **River banks** Rebecca G. aged 12

Q. What happened to the man that sat on the pin?

A. **He got the point** Rebecca G. aged 12

Q. What do you call a boomerang that doesn't come back?

A. **A stick**
Samuel S. aged 10

Q. Did you get the joke about the sun?

A. **No, I didn't, it was above my head**
Rebecca S. aged 10

Q. What do you call a goat with small knees?

A. **Kidneys**   Scott P. aged 9

Q. How many birthdays have you had?

A. **One, because you're only born once**   Lesley E. aged 11

Q. What did one candle say to the other candle?

A. **I'm going out tonight**   Jack M. aged 10

Q. Where do you find lots of keys that don't open anything?

A. **On a piano**
Mitchell J. aged 9

Q. How do you talk to a giant?

A. **You use big words**
Glen F. aged 7

31

Monday to Sunday

Each day is

an adventure

Each day is a fun day

So keep on laughing

From Monday to Sunday!

Q. What's the most boring day?

A. **Mun-day**
Aedan P. aged 10

Q. What's the best day to decide what to wear?

A. **Choose-day**
Kelly S. aged 12

Q. What's the best day to get married?

A. Wed-nesday Vanessa A. aged 12

Q What's the best day to drink orange juice?

A. Thirst-day Candice M. aged 12

Q. What is the best day to eat bacon and eggs?

A. Fry-day Wendy P. aged 12

Q. What's the best day to lounge around?

A. Sat-urday Lucille S.P. aged 12

Q. What's the best day for fathers and sons to get together?

A. Son-day Frank L. aged 12

Knock
Knock

There's a knock
on the door
And an answer — who's there?
It's bound to be funny —
Read on — if you dare!

Knock Knock

Who's there?

Oh no

Oh no who?

Oh no, I've got the wrong house

Sharnee B. aged 8

Knock Knock

Who's there?

Scott

Scott who?

Scott nothing to do with you

Kelvin H. aged 8

Knock Knock

Who's there?

Shirley

Shirley who?

Shirley I don't need to tell you

Fiona F. aged 10

Knock Knock

Who's there?

Who

Who who?

Are you an owl?

Dane T. aged 8

Knock Knock

Who's there?

Freeze

Freeze who?

Freeze a jolly good fellow

Peter G. aged 10

Knock Knock

Who's there?

Little old lady

Little old lady who?

I never knew you could yodel

Luke T. aged 9

Knock Knock

Who's there?

Theresa

Theresa who?

Theresa green

Jacob G. aged 10

Knock Knock

Who's there?

Omer

Omer who?

Omer goodness wrong door

Amber M. aged 9

Knock Knock

Who's there?

Mice

Mice who?

Mice to meet you

Nathan J. aged 8

Knock Knock

Who's there?

Cook

Cook who?

That's the first one I've heard this year   Fiona F. aged 10

Knock Knock

Who's there?

Amanda

Amanda who?

Amanda fix the TV

Ashton W. aged 11

Knock Knock

Who's there?

Ashley

Ashley who?

Ashley I want to play cards

Shannon B. aged 11

Knock Knock

Who's there?

Bok! Bok!

Bok! Bok! who?

Bok! Bok! I'm a chicken

Cassie W. aged 10

Knock Knock

Who's there?

Irish stew

Irish stew who?

Irish stew in the name of the law

Hope M. aged 12

Knock Knock

Who's there?

Abby

Abby who?

Abby Birthday

Melissa P. aged 10

Knock Knock

Who's there?

Iva

Iva who?

Iva sore hand from knocking on the door   Hayley N. aged 9

Funky
Monkeys

They hang from trees
And look real spunky
Those playful primates
The Funky Monkeys!

Q. Where do
monkeys cook
their toast?

A. **Under the
gorilla**
Brodie T. aged 8

Q. What do you
get if you cross
a gorilla and a
skunk?

A. **King Pong**
Scott G.aged 11

Q. What do you call a 2000 pound gorilla?

A. **Sir**
Dwayne S. aged 10

Q. Where do baby apes sleep?

A. **In apricots**
Brodie T. aged 10

Q. What do you call a gorilla with custard in one ear and jelly in the other?

A. **Anything you want, it can't hear you**
Nicola V.B. aged 10

Woos, Weaner, Wimp.

Q. What's pink and sticky and swings through the trees?

A. **A merangutan**
Joneen G. aged 11

Q. Why do gorillas have big fingers?

A. **Because they have big nostrils**
Sara B. aged 11

Furniture Follies

Look around the lounge room
And you'll get the jollies
The decor is funky
It's the Furniture Follies!

Q. What rocks and rolls but can't dance?

A. **A washing machine** Kitty K. aged 7

Q. What's Elvis Presley's favourite seat?

A. **A rockin' chair** Ellis S. aged 7

Q. What's the brightest baby in the house?

A. **A light bub** Amity V. aged 11

Q. What sort of table can you drink?

A. **A coffee table** Kelly P. aged 8

Q. What kind of furniture can you eat?

A. **Lounge sweets**
Becky F.
aged 8

Pretty
Kitty

Feline purring makes
Moggy ditties
Whiskers and milk
For Pretty Kitties

Q. What can cats have that dogs can't?

A. **Kittens**   Lauren W. aged 9

Q. What do you call a cat with no legs?

A. **Anything you like, it won't come anyway**
                                                    Natasha S. aged 12

Q. What is a cat's favourite sport?

A. **Puss-ups**   Kieren M. aged 6

Q. What do you get if you cross a cat with a grub?

A. **A caterpillar**   Renee G. aged 7

Q. What do you call a messy cat?

A. **Kitty Litter** Debra D. aged 8

Q. Why did the cat join St John's Ambulance?

A. **It wanted to be a first aid kit** Daniella O. aged 7

Q. Why are cats afraid to go outside?

A. **'Cause they're scaredy cats** Maddison T. aged 6

Q. Where do you find a new cat?

A. **In a catalogue** Stacey S. aged 8

Brain
Benders

Let's all share the pain
We're all mental members
Of the Kool Klub
The Incredible Brain Benders

Q. What do you call a bee born in May?

A. **A May-bee**   Claudia M. aged 6

Q. What has fingers but can't play the piano?

A. **A glove**   Rhia S. aged 9

Q. Why were there only 24 letters in the alphabet?

A. **Because U and I weren't there**   Hayley B. aged 12

Q. What do you do if you want to double your money?

A. **Fold it in half**
Lynette A. aged 10

Q. What did the biscuit say when another biscuit got run over by a car?

A. Crumbs! Jess M. aged 11

Q. How many sides does a circle have?

A. Two — one on the inside and one on the outside!
Brayden P. aged 9

Q. What has three eyes and one leg?

A. Traffic lights Brodie T. aged 10

Fly Swats

They fly around
And annoy you lots
The time has come
For Fly Swats!

Q. What did the fly say when he hit the window?

A. **If I had the guts I'd do that again**   Chris P. aged 12

Q. Where do flies do their shopping?

A. **Where they can get Fly Buys**   Selwyn B. aged 12

Blo-fli

Q. What do you call a fly without wings?

A. **A walk**   Jason A. aged 6

Q. Why did the fly fall off the wall?

A. **Because he had a fridge tied to his leg**
Damon B. aged 10

Twisted Tunes

You can sing to your budgie
You can sing to the moon
There's nothing like singing
The odd Twisted Tune

Q. What is a ram's favourite song?

A. **I'll Never Find Another Ewe**   Donna M. aged 9

Q. What type of pet has no eyes, legs and you never have to feed it?

A. **A trumpet**
Grace M. aged 11

Q. What's a heart's favourite song?

A. **The Beat Goes On**   Cassie P. aged 10

Q. What's a zebra's favourite song?

A. **The Lion Sleeps Tonight**   Anthony K. aged 9

Q. What type of phone never rings?

A. **A saxa-phone**   Kendall M. aged 7

Q. What is a pig's favourite instrument?

A. **A tam-boar-ine!**   Lenard Q. aged 9

One must ask
What's in a name?
Let's all play ...

The Name Game

Q. What do you call a man who grows herbs?

A. **Herbert**
Ellenor D. aged 9

Q. What do you call a man who likes fishing?

A. **Rod**
Reggie B. aged 12

Q. What do you call a woman who hangs out the washing?

A. **Peg**   Zane H. aged 12

Q. What do you call a man who likes the sun?

A. **Ray**   Ravi L. aged 10

Q. What do you call a woman who likes butter?

A. **Marj**   Francis F. aged 8

Q. What do you call a girl that likes jewellery?

A. **Jules**
Chris D. aged 10

Q. What do you call a woman who gets up early?

A. **Dawn**
Catherine B.M. aged 12

Q. What do you call a woman who mends fences?

A. **Barb**   Melanie L. aged 7

Q. What do you call a man with a car on his head?

A. **Jack**   Rebecca M. aged 10

Don't try this at home kids

Q. What do you call a girl with a frog on her head?

A. **Lilly**   Bree C. aged 9

Q. What do you call a woman who's good at saving money?

A. **Penny**   Stephen F. aged 10

Q. What do you call a girl traffic light?

A. **Amber**   Julie N.P. aged 6

Q. What do you call a man with a shovel?

A. **Doug**   Lorryndle E. aged 12

Traffic

Jams

Q. What kind of discos do traffic lights go to?

A. **Green light discos**
Abelle P. aged 11

Q. What's sweet and sticky and stops traffic?

A. **A traffic jam**
Justin R. aged 7

Q. Why did the chicken cross the road carrying a pair of scissors?

A. Because he wanted to cut corners　　Michelle D. aged 10

Q. What's an intersection's favourite ride?

A. A roundabout　　Lucy D. aged 12

Q. When do you get that run down feeling?

A. When you've been hit by a truck　Ryan G. aged 8

Q. Why did the computer cross the road?

A. The chook programmed it
Chris P. aged 12

They bark and ruff
And don't like moggies
Those canine jokers
The Dinky Doggies

Dinky Doggies

Q. What did the dog say when it sat on some sandpaper?

A. **Ruff Ruff**   Jade L. aged 12

Q. What do you call a dog that sits in the sun?

A. **A hot dog**   Chris K. aged 9

Q. What do you get if you cross a mutt with a poodle?

A. **A muddle**
Derek T. aged 8

Q. How does a hunter find his lost dog?

A. **He puts his ear to a tree and listens to the bark**
Adam T. aged 10

Q. What did the dog say when he burnt his tail?

A. **This is the end of me**
Amanda T. aged 10

Q. What do you get when you cross a skunk and a poodle?

A. **A smelly dog**
Emma R. aged 8

Q. What do you call a spaced-out dog?

A. **A pluto pup**
Amanda B. aged 8

Q. What do you call a poodle that can ski?

A. **A ski-doodle**
Kell R. aged 12

Ant-itude

In families of millions
It's hard to find food
For six-legged insects
With Ant-itude

Q. What do you call a really smart ant?

A. **Stud-ant**
Rachel P. aged 11

Q. Where do ants go for their holidays?

A. **Ant-arctica**
Bianca P. aged 10

Q. What do you call an ant in the army?

A. **Sergeant**
Debbie P. aged 9

Q. What do ants study at university?

A. **Ant-atomy**
Katrina B. aged 9

Q. What do you call
a really fat ant?

A. **An elephant**
Karen K. aged 10

Q. What do you call
an ant that won't
move?

A. **Stagnant**
Peter G. aged 9

Q. What's a really
happy ant?

A. **Exhuber-ant**
Josephine M. aged 8

Q. What sort of ant lives on your TV?

A **An antenna**
Mark A. aged 8

Q. What are the biggest ants in the world?

A. **Elephants!**
Kerry B. aged 6

Excellent
Elephants

Why did the elephant
cross the road
with the chook?
To read all the
jokes
In this red
hot book!

Q. What is grey, big and beautiful?

A. **Cinderelephant**   Samantha K. aged 10

Q. What did the elephant pack his clothes in?

A. **His trunk**   Janelle F.
   aged 5

Q. What do you get if you cross an elephant
   with a computer?

A. **A two-tonne know it all**
   Michael L.M. aged 11

Q. Why are elephants wrinkled?

A. **Have you ever tried ironing one?**
   Rhianna C. aged 10

Q. What do you give a sea-sick elephant?

A. **Lots of room**   Mitchell J. aged 9

Andy's Hot Shots

They're Hot and Kool
And always hit the spot
Andy's funky favourites
Super-Kool-Hot-Shots!

Q.   What is the Funky Monkey's favourite TV show?

A.   **The Groovy Moovy!**   Kaedyn H. aged 10

A schoolboy went to the teacher and said, "May I go to the bathroom?" The teacher answered, "First say the alphabet", so he started saying it:

"ABCDEFGHIJKLMNOQRSTUVWXYZ".

When the boy had finished the teacher asked, "What happened to the P?"

The boy looked down.

Caris M. aged 11

A man walked into a shop and asked for a fork. He got one.

Another man walked in and asked for a fork. He got one.

Then another man walked in and asked for a fork. He got one too.

Then another man walked in and asked for a straw.

"Why do you want a straw when everyone else wants a fork?"

The man answered, "Someone threw up on the sidewalk and all the chunky bits are gone."

Lauren M. aged 12

Jack: "I wish I had enough money to buy an elephant."

Jill: "Why do you want to buy an elephant?"

Jack: "I don't, I just wish I had the money."

Dylan O. aged 8

There were two men out fishing. Both were old and had false teeth. One man said to the other, "Oh no! I've lost my false teeth."

The other man thought this was funny and decided to play a trick on his friend, so he took his false teeth out and put them on the end of his fishing line and said to the other man, "Hey, look — I've caught your teeth on my line."

So the man who lost his teeth looked at them and said, "No, they're not my teeth" and threw them back in the water!

Tim S. aged 11

A flea walked into a milkbar, drank a milkshake and then walked out. Soon after he came back in.

"I thought you'd left," said the woman behind the counter.

The flea replied, "I did, but someone stole my dog!"

Natasha S. aged 12

A man was walking down a street with a penguin and a policeman came up and said, "Why don't you take that penguin to the zoo!" The man said, "What a good idea." The next day he was walking down the road with the penguin and the policeman came up and said, "I thought I told you to take that penguin to the zoo." The man said, "I did, and today I'm taking him to the movies!"

Regina W. aged 12

Sales Rep: "I keep logs on my travels."

Friend: "Oh really. I don't keep logs, I make them into furniture."

Simon C. aged 11

Son: "Dad, Dad, I came top in arithmetic today! The teacher asked what 3x15 was and I answered 42."

Father: "But that's wrong, the answer is 45."

Son: "I know, but I was closer than anyone else!"

Fiona F. aged 10

Andy's Top Ten

Words of wisdom
From young women and men
Best of the best
It's Andy's Top Ten

Q   Why couldn't James make an ice cube?

A   **Because he didn't know the recipe**   Elli I. aged 7

Mother: "What is the difference between an elephant's trunk and a postbox?"

Son: "I don't know."

Mother: "I won't send YOU to post my letters."

Marc A. aged 10

Q   How do you kiss
    a hockey player?

A   **You puck-er up**
    Claire L. aged 9

Q   Why is milk so fast?

A   **Because it's pasteurised before you see it**

Emma X. aged 10

Q What happens if your nose runs and your feet smell?

A **You've been turned upside down**
Claire L. aged 9

Q What happened to the boy who drank nine cokes?

A **He burped 7 up**
Jayden L. aged 8

Girl: "Are they braces you're wearing?"

Boy: "No, it's just a muzzle that keeps me from biting people who ask stupid questions."
Claudia L. aged 10

Q What has limbs but can't walk?

A **A tree**
Catiline M. aged 6

Q What happens when you go bald?

A **You have to carry your dandruff in your pocket**
Brian P. aged 8

Q What's green and eats porridge?

A **Mouldilocks**
Marc A. aged 10

Fly-Bye-Byes

It's jumbo jets and
Friendly skies
Let's take off with
Fly-Bye-Byes

Q How does an airline pilot's child say goodnight?

A **Goodnight Mummy, goodnight Daddy — over and out!**
Elizabeth S. aged 7

Q What is big, hairy and can fly?

A **King-Kong-corde**
Penelope F. aged 9

Q Why did the flying angel lose his job?

A **Because he had harp failure**
Hanson T. aged 10

Q What kind of dog can catch a plane?

A **A jet setter**
Mana F. aged 7

Q Where do birds invest their money?

A **In the stork market**
Sascha L. aged 6

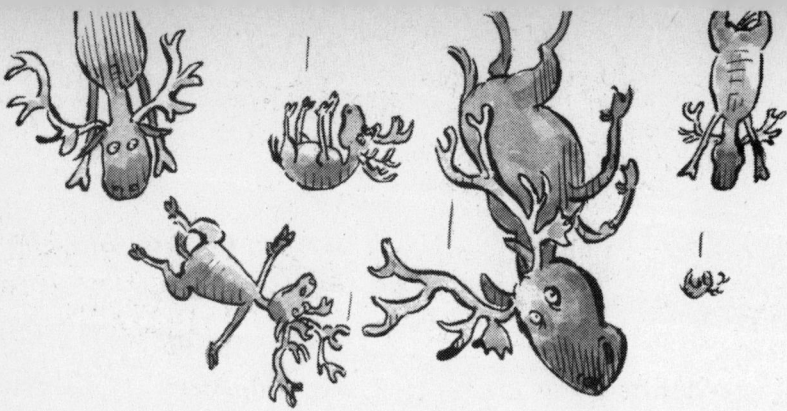

Q What animal drops from the clouds?

A **A raindeer**   Joe Q. aged 8

Q What do planes wear on their engines to keep them warm?

A **Jet-warmers**   Leigh B. aged 8

Q What do you call a plane that flies from point A to point B then back to point A?

A **A double crosser**   Lisa Y. aged 9

Q Why are planes good mimics?

A **Because they do great take offs**   Madlyn L. aged 7

Q Where do roosters go when they get to the airport?

A **The chick-in**   Lizzie C. aged 9

Hen Air

Q What happens if pigs fly?

A **Bacon goes up**   Seamus G. aged 9

Q What is the nicest plane in the world?

A **A Fokker Friendship**   Ryan S. aged 6

Q What do you call a plane that talks a lot?

A **A mumbo jumbo**   Huon F. aged 7

Q What is a rooster's favourite part of a plane?

A **The cock-pit**   Andy N. aged 9

Q What has two wings it can't flap, a beak it can't eat
   with and no feathers but can fly?

A **An aeroplane**   Nigel L. aged 10

Q What type of plane does E.T. fly on?

A **A jE.T.** _____   Dylan S. aged 9

Q What do you call a plane that fails to fly?

A **An aero-flop** Sandra P. aged 8

Q How do bank robbers escape by air?

A **They make a quick jetaway** Pauline W. aged 9

Q What do pilots do when they're bored?

A **Play aeronauts and crosses** Diana P. aged 7

Q How do you know when a pilot has a tummy upset?

A **He gets burpulence** Tim T. aged 6

Q Where do pilots go fishing?

A **In the jet stream** Tegan R. aged 9

Passenger: "I hope this plane doesn't travel faster than the speed of sound."
Flight attendant: "Why?"
Passenger: "Because my friend and I want to talk." Gillian T. aged 10

Body Parts

Double chins
And beating hearts
Piece 'em together
Body Parts

Q Why did the lady put lipstick on her head?

A **Because she wanted to make-up her mind** Gabriella B. aged 10

Q What do you call a sticky knee?

A **Hon-ey** Liam F. aged 5

Q What type of knee can you get at a bank?

A **Mon-ey** Ben H. aged 5

Q What do you call a knee which tells jokes?

A **Fun-ny** Madeleine L. aged 10

Q What type of room can you fit in your mouth?

A **A mushroom** Daniel S. aged 8

Q   What type of lids do you
     wear on your face?

A   **Eyelids**   Samuel T. aged 9

Q   What type of band can't play music?

A   **A hair band**   Prashad T. aged 8

Q   What type of stick can you put on your face?

A   **Lipstick**   Genevieve K. aged 7

Q   What do you call a baby knee?

A   **A mini**   Rhiannon L. aged 7

Q   What type of cage has no bars?

A   **A rib cage**   Joanne S. aged 9

Q   What do you call beautiful hands?

A   **Hand-some**   Kayla S. aged 8

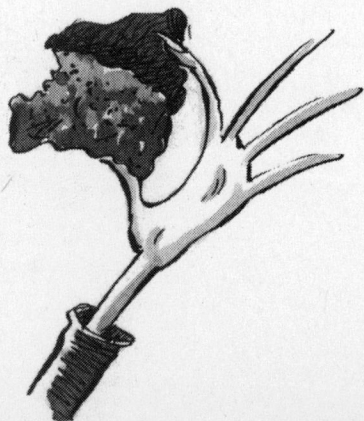

Q   Where do arms like to sit?

A   **In an armchair**   Rory F. aged 6

Q   What type of ribbon lives on your arm?

A   **An el-bow**   Tania B. aged 9

Q   What do you call a sleepy head?

A   **A bed-head**   Tania B. aged 9

Sizzling Hot Shots

Pots and cots
Knots and tots
Lots and lots of
Sizzling Hot Shots

Q What has a neck but no head?

A **A bottle**   Vanessa T. aged 11

Q Why is a rabbit's nose always shiny?

A **Because the powder puff is at the wrong end**   Lauren A. aged 7

Q What nut sounds like a sneeze?

A **A cashew**   Pepe S. aged 6

Q What is a complete waste of time?

A **Telling a hair-raising story to a bald man**

Daniel F. aged 10

Q Where do sheep cook their meat?

A **On a Baa-b-que**

Mitchell H. aged 10

Q If two's company and three's a crowd, what are four and five?

A **Nine**
Louis B. aged 6

Q Why is tennis a noisy game?

A **When you play it you have to raise a racket**
Jessica B. aged 6

Q What runs but has no legs?

A **A tap**
Hayden T. aged 8

Q What did the farmer say when he saw his cow in a tree?

A **"Get down!"**
Stephanie L. aged 9

Keys Please

There's lots of fun
In riddles like these
But they're hard to unravel
Pass the Keys Please!

Q   What type of key can you wipe your nose with?

A   **A han-key**   Matthew S. aged 9

Q   What do you call a beautiful key?

A   **Spun-key**   Elizabeth P. aged 10

Q   What do you call a long key?

A   **Lan-key**   Shelley K. aged 7

Q   What do you call a grumpy key?

A   **Sul-key**   Kristina R. aged 9

Q   What do you call a key that wins you money?

A   **Luc-key**   Ariadne A. aged 6

Q   What do you call an angry key?

A   **Cran-key**   Genevieve M. aged 9

Q   What sort of food do keys eat?

A   **Bic-keys**   Helena B. aged 9

Q   What do you call a key in a leather jacket?

A   **A bi-key**   James E. aged 6

Q   What country do keys come from?

A   **Tur-key**   Luke S. aged 7

Q   What does a key wear to the beach?

A   **A bi-key-ni**   Ryan T. aged 8

African Animals

Hanging from trees
Dining with cannibals
They're so exotic
African Animals

Q What do you call a rhinoceros who swings through the trees?

A **A vinoceros**
Susan S. aged 7

Q Why does a giraffe have a long neck?

A **Because he can't stand the smell of his feet**
Casey C. aged 7

Q   Where did Tarzan buy his clothes?

A   **At a jungle sale**   Jane S. aged 7

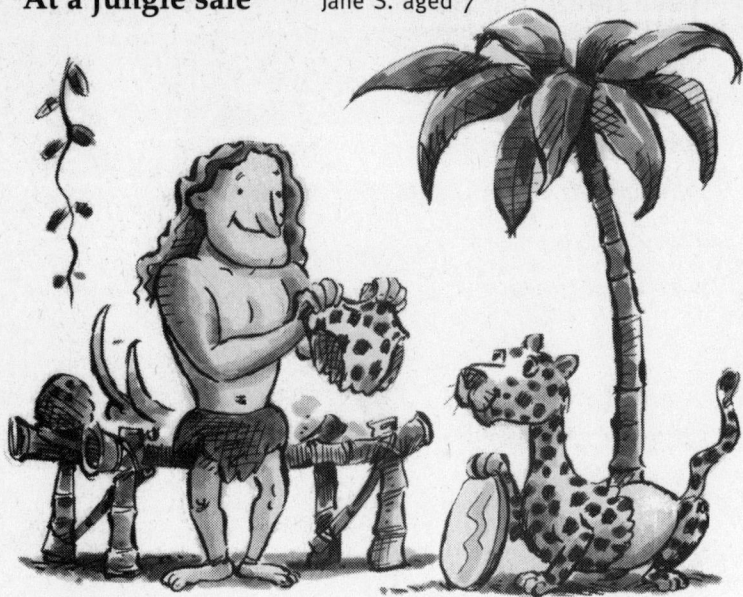

Q   What kind of monkey can fly?

A   **A hot air baboon**   Dean T. aged 8

Q   What is pretty, has big teeth and flies?

A   **A killer butterfly**   Joe S. aged 8

Q   Why couldn't the leopard escape from the zoo?

A   **Because he was always spotted**   Adam J. aged 9

Q   What is hairy and coughs?

A   **A coconut with a cold**
Benjamin S. aged 9

Q   What do cannibals have for lunch?

A   **Baked beings**   Kayleigh C. aged 8

Q   What should you do for a starving cannibal?

A   **Give him a hand**   Vicki W. aged 7

Q   What do cannibals eat for breakfast?

A   **Buttered host**   Chamberlain Y. aged 8

Q   What do you call a really messy hippo?

A   **A hippopota-mess**   James J. aged 10

Q   What's the largest mouse in the world?

A   **A hippopota-mouse**

Lydia T. aged 7

Q   Which animal is always laughing?

A   **A happy-potamus**   Jane R. aged 7

Q   What do you call an out-of-breath mammoth?

A   **An ele-pant**   Caren R. aged 6

Q   What's tall and smells nice?

A   **A Giraff-o-dill**   Shani R. aged 7

Q   What is striped and goes around and around?

A   **A zebra in a revolving door**   Anna S. aged 9

Q   What swings through the
    trees and is very
    dangerous?

A   **A chimpanzee with a
    machine gun**
    Vince S. aged 10

What a Load of Croc!

Menacing reptiles
And jaws that lock
Gnawing of funny bones
What a Load of Croc!

Q   How do you phone up a croc?

A   **You croc-a-dial**   Chris A. aged 9

Q   What do you get if you cross a rooster with a
    crocodile?

A   **A croc-a-doodle-doo**   Joanna H. aged 10

Q   What time is it when you meet a crocodile?

A   **Time to run**   Freya O. aged 9

Q   What do crocodiles cook their food in?

A   **Croc pots**   Ingrid M. aged 7

Q   What do you call a crocodile that goes door to door?

A   **A sales rep-tile**   Andrew M. aged 10

Computer Chips

*Games and screensavers
And electronic blips
They all run on
Computer Chips*

Q   Where do computers go to dance?

A   **The disk-o**   Michael O. aged 8

Q   When is a key-bored?

A   **When it is with a computer**   Thomas P. aged 8

Q   What is a computer's favourite animal?

A   **A mouse**   James P. aged 10

Q   What do all computers look through?

A   **Windows**   Troy R. aged 8

Q   What do you call a high-voltage computer?

A   **An AC-DC PC**   Brent O. aged 10

Q   How do computers catch fish?

A   **In-ter-net**   Matthew O. aged 10

Q How do you know when a computer wants to stay over?

A **It wants to DOS**   Adrian M. aged 10

Q What's the difference between a boxer and a computer?

A **You only need to punch information into a computer once**   Benjamin K. aged 9

Q How do you know when a computer is tired?

A **It takes floppy disks**
Jessica R. aged 6

Q   What do you get when you cross 2000 smarties and a computer?

A   **A multi-coloured smarty party**   Danielle K. aged 8

Q   How do computers go through a divorce?

A   **They Control-Alt-Delete**   Jenna S. aged 10

Q   What do you call a gorgeous computer?

A   **A QT PC**   Brittany C. aged 10

Songs of the Sea

Listen up me hearties
Wherever you be
To these wet and wild
Songs of the Sea

Q   What does a deaf fisherman need?

A   **A herring aide**   Margaret W. aged 9

Q   What kind of cat lives in the ocean?

A   **An octo-pus**   Jack B. aged 7

Q   How do you make a goldfish old?

A   **Take away the G**   Robert D. aged 7

Q What do you call a really quiet fish?

A **A shh...shh...shark** Nicola R. aged 8

Q Where do dead fish swim?

A **In the Dead Sea** Suzie S. aged 9

Q Where do seagulls rest at sea?

A **On a perch** Matt C. aged 6

Q What type of fish is best eaten at the beginning of the week?

A **Barra-Monday** Mane C. aged 7

Q   What do you call an angry fish?

A   **Snapper**   Nicholas E. aged 9

Q   What do you get if you
      jump in the Red Sea?

A   **Wet**   Lucas B. aged 9

Q   How do you make a sea creature rich?

A   **Take the S out of squid — quid**   Ciara C. aged 8

Q   What did one rockpool say to the other?

A   **Show us your mussels**   Matthew C. aged 7

Q   What dives under the sea and carries 64 people?

A   **An octo-bus**   Justin R. aged 7

Q   What do you call a baby whale?

A   **A little squirt**   Christopher M. aged 9

Q   What is a shark's favourite vegetable?

A   **A crab-bage**

Kristina B. aged 9

Q   What do you call a sea mammal in pain?

A   **A squeal**

Michael L. aged 10

Q   What do mermaids eat for breakfast?

A   **Mermalade on toast**

Emma P. aged 6

Feathered Funnies

They're not clucking horses
Or quacking bunnies
But they tweet and they crow
They're the Feathered Funnies

Q   What do ducks watch on TV?

A   **Duckumentaries**   Ashleigh R. aged 8

Q   What goes cluck cluck bang?

A   **A chicken in a minefield**   Timothy M. aged 7

Q   What did the magpie say to the scarecrow?

A   **I'll knock the stuffing out of you**   Nathan S. aged 9

Q What is the most common illness in birds?

A **Flu** William T. aged 7

Q Why does Batman look for worms?

A **To feed his Robin** Julian P. aged 8

Q What bird is always laughing?

A **A kooky-burra** Adam W. aged 6

The Big Budgie Ball

Q What did the owl say after the square dance?

A **That was a hoot** Laura N. aged 7

Q When is the best time to buy budgies?

A **When they are going cheep** Denis A. aged 11

Q What do you get if you cross a bird with a fly?

A **A fly-fly** Holly J. aged 6

Q   What do chickens expect at the theatre?

A   **Hentertainment**   Martin B. aged 8

Q   How did the exhausted sparrow land safely?

A   **By sparrow-chute**   Jack J. aged 7

Q   What are feathers good for?

A   **Birds**   April F. aged 9

Q   Where do sparrows go on holidays?

A   **Sparrow-dice**   Sam Q. aged 7

Q   How do sparrows tell the future?

A   **Sparrow cards**   Lisa F. aged 10

You will meet a short brown stranger

Q   What do you get if you run over a sparrow with a lawn mower?

A   **Shredded tweet**

Jordan D. aged 7

oops

Q   What do you call a pig that flies?

A   **A pig-eon**   Margi R. aged 9

Q   What kind of pie can fly?

A   **A magpie**

Michelle S. aged 7

Miraculous Mothers

A reassuring hug
That's better than all others
They're the best
Miraculous Mothers

Q   What's a mother's favourite jam?

A   **Mama-lade**   Holly F. aged 6

Q   What do you get if you cross a mother with a lot of humps?

A   **Mumps**   Caitlin L. aged 7

Q   What do you call a big mum?

A   **Maxi-mum**   Andrew E. aged 8

Q   What do you call a little mum?

A   **Mini-mum**   Andrew E. aged 8

Q What did the hungry shark say when he saw a mother swimming?

A Mmm... A yummy mummy   Samuel S. aged 8

Q What do you call a mummy who sings in the shower?

A A hummy   Isaac L. aged 9

Q What do you call a mother with bread on her lap?

A A crumby mummy   Jessica B. aged 6

Q   What does your mother use to buy food?

A   **Mum-ney**   Paul R. aged 7

Q   What's a mother's favourite day of the week?

A   **Mumday**   Amelia T. aged 5

Q   What's a mother's favourite fruit?

A   **A bamama**   Sophie S. aged 5

Whacky Wally

For clever conversation
Talk to Pretty Polly
But if you want a giggle
Just watch Whacky Wally

Q   What do you call a wally in a clothes drier?

A   **A whirly**   Ian M. aged 7

Q   What do you call a wally on the wing of a jet?

A   **A windy**   Katie S. aged 9

Q   How do you get a one-armed wally out of a tree?

A   **Wave to him**   Pia K. aged 9

Q Where do wallies go for holidays?

A **Wally World**
Nikki B. aged 7

Q What do you get if you cross a clown, Sherlock Holmes and a wally?

A **A jolly wally, by golly**
Gina S. aged 6

Q What do you get if you cross a wally with a parrot?

A **A polly wally**
Gabriel M. aged 8

Q Why did the wally fall out of the tree?

A **Because he was tied to a koala**
Helen V. aged 6

Eskimos-es

Igloo gags
And a rub of noses
The North Pole houses
Eskimos-es!

Q What's an Eskimo's favourite car?

A **An Eskimoke**   Con V. aged 9

Q What do Eskimos do before they kiss?

A **They ug**   Anna S. aged 6

Q How do you keep an Eskimo cold?

A **Take away the "mo"**   Aimee I. aged 7

Q What do you call an Eskimo that asks questions?

A **An Askimo**   James T. aged 10

Q How do Eskimos hold their homes together?

A **Ig-glue**   Louisa M. aged 8

Q   What do old Eskimos eat?

A   **Seals on Wheels**   Karly S. aged 6

Q   What do Eskimos wear on their heads?

A   **Polar hair**   James L. aged 7

Q   How do you know when two Eskimos are in love?

A   **They get nosy**   Josephine M. aged 9

Q   What falls at the North Pole but never gets hurt?

A   **Snowflakes**   Talia M. aged 7

Q   How do Eskimos transport snails?

A   **Es-cargo**   Georgia V. aged 9

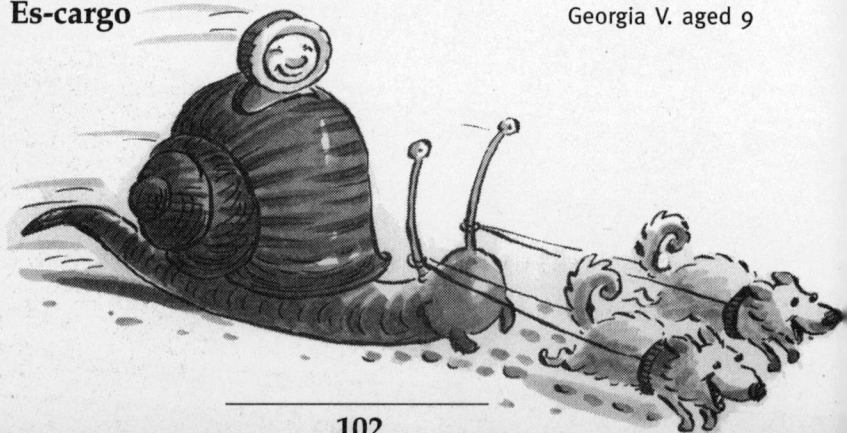

Aussie Knock Knocks

Emus and koalas
Oceans and rocks
A joke book's not fair dinkum
Without Aussie Knock Knocks

Knock Knock

Who's there?

Cargo

Cargo who?

Cargo beep beep

Thomas L. aged 6

Knock Knock

Who's there?

Alison

Alison who?

Alison to the radio

Thomas L. aged 6

Knock Knock

Who's there?

Mister

Mister who?

Mister last train home

Billy M. aged 7

Knock Knock

Who's there?

My panther

My panther who?

My panther falling down Marny S. aged 8

Knock Knock

Who's there?

Ammonia

Ammonia who?

Ammonia little boy Lisa K. aged 7

Knock Knock

Who's there?

Vegemite

Vegemite who?

Vegemite not taste so good Diana P. aged 7

Knock Knock

Who's there?

Saul

Saul who?

It's Saul over Peter T. aged 8

Knock Knock

Who's there?

Romeo

Romeo who?

Rome-over to the other side of the lake Peter T. aged 8

Knock Knock

Who's there?

Bed

Bed who?

Bedder late than never

Danielle M. aged 7

Knock Knock

Who's there?

Wombats

Wombats who?

Wombat's better than none

Brenda V. aged 9

Knock Knock

Who's there?

Dingo

Dingo who?

Dingo anywhere on the weekend

Thomas C. aged 7

Knock Knock

Who's there?

Emu

Emu who?

Emu all along

Bradley S. aged 8

Knock Knock

Who's there?

Caterpillar

Caterpillar who?

Cat-er-pillar of feline society

Mark L. aged 10

Knock Knock

Who's there?

Outback

Outback who?

Out back you'll find a rock

Guy S. aged 8

Knock Knock

Who's there

Kanaroo

Kanaroo who?

Kanaroo jump a six-foot fence?

Charlotte F. aged 9

Knock Knock

Who's there?

Koala

Koala who?

Koala Lumpur is not in Australia

Daisy F. aged 10

Knock Knock

Who's there?

Dubbo

Dubbo who?

Dub-bo fires the arrow

Alexis P. aged 7

Knock Knock

Who's there?

Adelaide

Adelaide who?

Adel-laide the snags on the barbie

Samantha T. aged 9

Knock Knock

Who's there?

Canberra

Canberra who?

Can-berra lot more than you think

Michelle T. aged 9

Knock Knock

Who's there?

Barbecue

Barbecue who?

**Barbecue for the
pool table, please**

Liam D. aged 10

Knock Knock

Who's there?

Footy

Footy who?

Foo-ty I'd like fish fingers please

Kym R. aged 9

Knock Knock

Who's there?

Cossie

Cossie who?

Cos-sie I'm a little confused by this

Georgia E. aged 9

Knock Knock

Who's there?

Coogee

Coogee who?

Coogee coogee coo

Kayla F. aged 7

Knock Knock

Who's there?

Yabbie

Yabbie who?

Ya-bbie a crayfish, man

Michelle F. aged 7

Flower Power

Wattles and waratahs
And gladioli tower
A rainbow of colour
It's Flower Power

Q How do you recognise a flower in a speedway?

A **They put the petal to the metal**   Joshua S. aged 7

Q What kind of flower shows off all the time?

A **A posy**   Eric B. aged 8

Q Where do flowers go on holidays?

A **Gardenia**   Oliver C. aged 6

Q Why did the ivy cry?

A **Cause it weed**   Harriet T. aged 9

Q What do you call a strange plant?

A **A weed-o** Andrew F. aged 8

Q What do you call an old flower?

A **Poppy** Max E. aged 7

Q What do you call a stupid flower?

A **A daffy-dill** Kayleigh C. aged 7

Q What type of tree can sit in your hand?

A **A palm tree** Hannah L. aged 6

Q What do you call a flower that bites its lip?

A **A tulip** Angela S. aged 9

Q What do you call a tree you can't find?

A **A mys-tree** Sonia R. aged 8

Thundering Underwear

Bloomers and boxers
Undergarments with flair
There is nothing as silly
As Thundering Underwear

Q What type of undies do scarecrows wear?
A **Wicker knickers**   Nicholas F. aged 7

Q What kind of underwear do bees wear?
A **Underbear**   Tyson P. aged 9

Q What type of undies do teachers wear?
A **Und-Ds**   Christian J. aged 8

Q What type of underwear packs a punch?
A **Boxer shorts**   Tina W. aged 9

Q What never sleeps and constantly needs changing?
A **A nappy**   Stan D. aged 9

Q   What do baby crabs wear?

A   **Nippy nappies**   Zoe Y. aged 8

Q   What did one pair of underpants say to the other?

A   **I need a change**   Kimberley R. aged 9

Q   What is a musician's favourite undergarment?

A   **A G-string**   Laura P. aged 9

Q   What is the best day of the week to change your underwear?

A   **Mundie**   Kenneth C. aged 7

Outback 'n' Beyond

There's roos and wombats
And a cane toad in a pond
There's a Budgee from Mudgee
Outback 'n' Beyond

Q   What do you call 50 kangaroos running across the Harbour Bridge?

A   **An illusion**   Emily F. aged 7

Q   What kind of bat can't fly?

A   **A wombat**   Catherine S. aged 9

Wow!... Heavy, man.

Q   What do you call a kangaroo that lives in Nimbin?

A   **A hoppy hippy**   Carmel B. aged 7

Q   What do you get if you cross a kangaroo and a cow?

A   **A kanga-moo**   Steven P. aged 7

Q   What do you get if you cross a kangaroo with a
    farmer?

A   **A jackaroo**   Brian W. aged 9

Q   When does an emu become a sheep?

A   **When you remove the "em"**   David L. aged 8

Q   What was the first Australian musical instrument?

A   **A ridgy didge**   Kylie B. aged 9

Q   What do you call a bird from Mudgee?

A   **A budgee**   Paul L. aged 6

Q   What did the cane toad
    say when he saw a
    bunny run by?

A   **Rabbit, rabbit**
    Angus N. aged 7

Q   What's a kangaroo's
    favourite music?

A   **Hip hop**
    Oscar C. aged 9

Chocolate Treats

It's the fabulous flavour
That nothing beats
We love to eat 'em
Chocolate Treats

Q What's an astronaut's favourite food?

A **A Mars Bar**   Thomas L. aged 8

Q What's white and brown and goes to the movies?

A **A choc top**   Robert F. aged 9

Q What type of chocolates live on rocks?

A **Oyster eggs**   Gabrielle D. aged 7

Q   What did the chocolate say to the lollipop?

A   **See you later sucker**   Adrian L. aged 8

Q   How do you stop someone eating your last chocolate?

A   **Eat it first**   Blair P. aged 8

Preposterous Pets

No matter how silly
Your dog or cat gets
It couldn't compare to
These Preposterous Pets

Q What type of animal eats crumbs?

A **A crum-pet**
Hank M. aged 9

Q How do you start an animal race?

A **Ready, pet-ty, go**
Joshua C. aged 7

Q What type of animal eats cars and covers your floor?

A **A car-pet**
Rory T. aged 6

Q What do you call a bunch of protesting animals?

A **A pet-ition**
Kit F. aged 9

Q What do you call an animal that whinges about small things?

A **Pet-ty**

Jackson C. aged 6

Terrific Teachers

Although they can be
Scary creatures
Still we love our
Terrific Teachers

G'day Sir Whaddar youse doin' ere?

There was a knock at the front door.

A little boy opened it.

"Are your parents in?" asked his teacher.

"They was in," answered the boy. "But they is out now."

"They was in, they is out now!" exclaimed the teacher. "Where is your grammar?"

The boy answered, "In the front room watching telly."

Rosie B. aged 10

Teacher: "If I gave you three rabbits and then the next day I gave you two more rabbits, how many would you have?"

Boy: "Six, Miss."

Teacher: "Six?"

Boy: "Yes, Miss, I've already got one."   Alistair M. aged 7

Teacher: "Johnny, have you decided what you would like to do when you finish school?"

Johnny: "Yes, Miss, I would like to follow the medical profession."

Teacher: "So you want to be a doctor?"

Johnny: "No, Miss, an undertaker!"   Hailey C. aged 11

Son: "Mum, I don't want to go to school — the teacher hates me and so do the children."

Mum: "You have to go, darling, you're the principal."

Silly Situations

They're enough to
Try your patience
Absolutely absurd,
Silly Situations

An apprentice butcher had been sacked for incompetence and vowed revenge on his employer.

The following Saturday morning, when the shop was packed with people buying meat, he marched in, elbowed his way to the counter and slapped down one very dead cat.

"There you are, Mr Smith," he called out cheerily. "That makes up the dozen you ordered."

B.J.Ryan aged 10

A man asked his boss if he could have an hour off to get his hair cut.

"Certainly not," said the boss, and suggested he have it cut in his own time.

"But it grows when I'm at work," the man said.

The boss replied, "It doesn't do all its growing during work hours, you know."

The man said, "Well I'm not having it all off!"

Jason P. aged 10

Boss: "You're late for work again."

Worker: "Yes, I'm sorry — I overslept."

Boss: "I thought I told you to get an alarm clock."

Worker: "I did, but there are nine of us in our family."

Boss: "What's that got to do with it?"

Worker: "The alarm was only set for eight!"

Kimberley J. aged 10

Two old men were sitting outside a milk bar with a dog resting at their feet.

One man asked, "Does your dog bite?"

The other man answered, "No."

The first man bent down to pat the dog and the dog bit his arm off.

"I thought you said your dog doesn't bite."

"That's not my dog!"

Casey S. aged 10

Applicant: "I've come about the handyman job."

Employer: "Are you handy?"

Applicant: "Couldn't be handier."

Employer: "How so?"

Applicant: "I live next door!"

Kerrin R. aged 10

A jumbo jet was flying over central Australia when an announcement came over the intercom:

"Ladies and gentleman, I must inform you that one of our engines has failed. Don't worry; we still have three engines working properly. We will be delayed by one hour, though."

A few minutes later the captain came on again, and said, "We have lost another engine but can still run on two, though we will now be two hours late."

Shortly after the captain came on again. "I do apologise, we have lost another engine — but the aircraft can fly perfectly well on one engine, although we'll be three hours late."

One passenger turned to another and said: "I hope we don't lose that last one, otherwise we'll be here all day."

Kevin C. aged 12

Once upon a time there were three little pigs.

The first little pig came into the bar and asked for a lemonade. After drinking it he asked where the toilet was. "Down the hall to the left," the barman replied. So the little pig went off to the toilet.

Soon a second little pig came and asked for a lemonade, then asked the barman where the toilet was. Once again the barman said, "Down the hall to the left."

Then the third little pig came in and asked for a lemonade. When he had finished drinking it the barman asked, "Don't you want to know where the toilet is?" The pig answered, "No I'm the little pig that went wee, wee, wee all the way home." Laura C. aged 8

A horse walked into a bar and the barman asked: "Why the long face?"
Amy N. aged 8

Published by ABC Books for the
AUSTRALIAN BROADCASTING CORPORATION
GPO Box 9994 Sydney NSW 2001

First published October 2002
Reprinted October 2002

National Library of Australia
Cataloguing-in-Publication entry
Bumper book of hot jokes for kool kids volume two.

ISBN 0 7333 1115 6

1. Riddles, Juvenile. 2. Wit and humor, Juvenile. I.
Axelsen, Stephen. II. Jones, Andy, 1961- . III. Australian Broadcasting
Corporation. IV. Title : Red hot jokes for kool kids. V. Title : Sizzling hot
jokes for kool kids.
A828.302

Designed by Marius Foley Graphic Design
Illustrated by Stephen Axelsen
Set in Palatino 12pt by Marius Foley Graphic Design
Colour separations by Colorwize, Adelaide
Printed and bound by Griffin Press, Adelaide.

5 4 3 2